LEARNING
ACHIEVING
DREAM
METHODS

JOHN LOK

Contents

Preface

Introduction

I write this book aims to let readers to understand whether what the actual factors can cause dream to achieve easily as well as what factors must help us to achieve successful or failure in our career plan. Ane one must have dream, e.g. business owner or founder or individual professional, even he/she feels his/her dream is difficult to achieve. However, I believe that his/her dream must have some factors may help him/her to achieve easily. What are the main elements to help any one to achieve dream successfully. What are the measurement methods to judge that the person can achieve his/her life aim successfully. I hope that my readers can make reasonable judgement whether what factors may help you to achieve any dreams to implement successfully. In my this book, I shall indicate both dreams, one is sport athlete career and business founder career how you can may achieve these both dreams easily.

Prologue

Table of content

CHAPTER ONE

Business founder dream

Any successful business founder must need have good business strategy or business plan in order to achieve his/her business runs long time. I shall explain how business strategy and business plan are the main factors to influence any one business founder achieves successful business dream as below:

Why do new businesses need business plans or strategies? How can any kinds of business plans and strategies help new businesses development? If business plan will be used primarily to get funding for the venture or direct the operation. So, the two plans and targeting different timeframes in a business history . The different design of business plan and strategy mus be the main factors to influence any businesses to run long time , business plan is in the beginning of the new business, business strategy is the running of the new business. A strategic plan is used to investigate a future period, usually between three to five years.

Hence, the function of business plan , it can help the business founder to define and classify the goals he has to achieve his new business. A good business plan is a business document that is written for a variety of audiences. The business founder might send his business plan to investors or it might be written for the benefit of his employees. Otherwise, the function of strategic plan , it purposes to set overall goals for the business founder and to develop a plan to achieve them. It involves stepping bank from his day-to-day operations and asking where his new busines is needed and what its priorities should be , for business function strategies example, they need to improve implementation of business and corporate strategies. Functions strategies include marketing strategies, and human resource strategies, often they concern specifics, such as resource strategies often they concern specifics, such as resource allocation, operation expense, efficiencies and product improvement.

So, a strategic plan is primarily used for implementing and managing the strategies direction of an existing organization. A business plan is used to intially start a business, obtain funding or direct operations. Whereas, a business plan is used to provide a structure for ideas in order to initially define the business. So, the main three purposes of a business plan, it creates an effective strategy for growth to determine future financial needs and to attract investors and lenders. The five elements of an annual business plan may include: Situation analysis, it means that a situation analysis defines the current situation and must be an objective assessment, the market analysis, it is an indepth assessment of competition and competitors marketing strategy, positioning to new product or service, setting short term , middle term and long term objectives , choice the most useful or effective strategies.

In long organizations , they will need business plans and strategic planning. So, strategic planning is an organizational management activity that is used to set priorities, focus energy and resources, strengthen operations, ensure that employers and other stakeholders are working toward common goals, establish agreement around intended outcomes/results and access and adjust the organiztations aims and performance, whether its performance is achieved to the most satisfactory level. Hence, the five steps for strategic planning may include: Determine strategic position, prioritize objectives, develop a strategic plan, executive and manage plan and review and revise the plan.

The value of strategic planning may bring these benefits: Assisting the management team on a stratetgic agenda to move the organization toward, communicate clarity of direction throughout the organization, provide clear direction and restore integrity of leadership, and solve key performance problems.

However, in any large organizations, they may have these 3 levels of strategy: corporate level strategy, this level answers the foundational question of what the business founder want to achieve, business unit level strategy, this level focuses on how new business is going to corporate , marketing level strategy focuses on how new business is going to grow. In business environment, any large organizations must have these four main functional areas. So, business leaders, e.g. CEO feel that they need to prepare good business plans or strategies in order to satisfy their four main organizational function development. The four main functions may include: marketing, human resource, operation and finance. For a fuinctional strategy example, it is concerned with different functional areas in an organization., These include technology, marketing, finance etc. There are six fiunctional areas in an organization, they may include : Strategy , marketing, finance, human resource, technology and equipment and operation. For five ps of strategy may include: plan, ploy, pattern, position and perspective. For 5 business level strategies may also include: cost leadership, differentiation, integrated low cost differentiation, focused differentiation, focused low cost.

Thus, choice which one business level strategy , it depends on whether what kind of business and who are its competitors' marketing strategy, for example, China or US country, they have less number of gas product firms, because gas firms' oil products are similar , so they are difficult to sell different kinds of gas product. They will choose low cost or low sale price strategy, e.g. reducing gas sale price in season period, or choose cheap gas manufacture material in order to reduce manufacturing cost. So, focused low cost strategy may be general gas organizations.

However, there are general kinds of business strategies to large new organizational development, e.g. cross-sell more products , cheap warehouse product , most innovated product or service, e.g. smart phone or laptop products, grow sales from new products, e.g. non-manual auto cars, improve customer service, e.g. airline e-ticket online purchase, e-commerce sale organization, concerning a young market, e.g. clother , sport shoe etc. product differentiation, e.g. different kinds of new furniture design, pricing strategies, e.g. seasonal cheap car gas , reducing car gas price for half year, technological advantages, e.g. air fresh machine innovation, it aims to avoid air pollution in factory manufacturing environment or any working environment for business users.

However, in general, any large organizations also need to

prepare business plan in order to achieve their objectives, the 4 types of business plan may include: operational plan, it is about how things need to happen, motivational leadership, otherwise, strategic plans are all about why things need to happen as well as tactical planning and contingency planning.

The most important part of business plan concerns the executive summary and perhaps the only one that will get need to make it perfect. The executive summary has only one objective, it aims to attract the investor to read the new organization's full business plan report in order to persuade he accepts the founder's new business investment aim. The four elements of a business plan may include: the executive summary, marketing plan, key management, nios and financial plan business plan sections are critical and should be included in all business plans additional section can be added to these four when targeting specific purposes and audiences. The seven parts of business plan may include: executive summary, company description, introduction of new product, and service, market analysis , strategy and implementation, organization and management team, financial plan.

However, the steps of the strategic management process for any kinds of stragegy plan implementation, they may include these steps: step 1 review or develop vision and mission, step 2 business and operation analysis (SWOT analysis etc.) step 3 develop and select strategic options, step 4 establish strategic objectives, step 5 strategic execution plan, step 6 establish resource allocation, step 7 executive review., All of these steps must need to any large organizations , when they prepare to implement any right management strategy to run their new businesses . These strategic planning processes may include environmental scanning of gathering, organizing and analyzing information .

Strategy formulation implementation and evaluation . Hence, any organizations hope to achieve an effective strategy, strategic effectiveness is an organization's ability to set the right goals and consistently achieve them. There is a clear hierarchy in levels of strategy, with corporate level strategy at the top, business level strategy being derived from the corporate level and the functional level strategy being formulated out of the business level strategy, e.g. client event strategy is designed to improve client satisfaction . Hence, when the large organization can prepare a good business plan to know how to run its new business, then it will decide how to choose its the most right strategy to implement its new business operation more easily and successfully.

CHAPTER TWO

Attempting to learn failure experiences to bring success

I believe that any one successful person, he / she must have same personal characteristrics. They can accept to attempt to choose to do any new career decision. They wil not afraid failure, they feel that failure experiences may help them to bring learning new career experiences chance. So, they believe that any failure carrer experiences may help them to reach successful aims more easily.

I shall indicate some successful business founders to explain what why they may attempt to acept new chance, although their these new career decisions may being failure possible risks. But, they do not feel fear to their new career choice risks. Consequently, their choices may help them to bring present busines success. I shall indicate these two successful business Fonders. They are IBM Microsoft founder Bill and Amazon founder.

In their past business development careers, they have similar career choice experiences. IBM Microsoft founder forgave his computer science undergraduate degree to continue to pursue to study. So, he could not graduate computer science degrss in US one university. In fact, his decision may bring risk because he can not graduate this computer science degree. In 1980 year, computer industry began to develop. If he can graduate the computer science degree, he oughr find any computer programmer job to earn good salary.

What reason influenced he forgave to continue to continue to learn in university? The reason is simple because IBM MIcrosoft founder believes that it is right time ro apply his US university computer lectuer teaches his computer science knowledge to invent computer software new product. He beleived that his new computer software invention can help global students to apply computers to learn or do homeworks. So, global any one student can buy one computer at home. His / her computer is needed to apply Microsoftware to turn on. So, IBM Microsoft founder must have more confidnece to his software must be future any computer essential machine part. Any computers can not apply his Microsoftware to turn on computes successfully. So, Microsoftware became loyalty to earn more income. Microsoft founder can attempt to accept fail because he will lose his computer science degree graduation chance as well as he will have chance to fail to invent his software new computer product both. However, he proves that he can succeed to invent his microsoftware. Even, he had began to run his IBM Microsoftware to still to global office and student and family computer users in popular. Moreover, any computer manufacturers must need Microsoftware to turn on their computer products. So, any computer manufacturers must need to buy Microsoftware products to help them to turn on their computer products equipment sucessully. It mean that Microsoftware is essential part to any nowadays computers. SO, IBM founder can earn each one computer software royalty income from global any one computer manufacturer. Sp. it explains that why IBM founder can beomce rich businessman.

However, IBM founder;s successful main factor, is due to his acceptance of learning new career experience. Before he planned to finish his computer science degree to seek general computer programmer job to become computer programmer professional in any organizations. But when IBM founder believed that his new MIcrosoftware product invention may succeed to bring clerical tasks advantages to global any one student or office or family computer users. So, he decided to forgave his further computer science degree to pursue computetr programmer professional career. He chooses to attempt to be one computer software product inventor , even business founder to develop his business career.

IN fact, IBM founder must have risk, if ha can not succeed to invent his new computer software product. Then , he can not be one inventor, even he can not achieve his new computer software product invention dream successfully. Hence, he must experience to worry about whether his software invention can success. However, he does not fear to failure. He believes that he must succeed to invent computer software product to supply to future global any one computer for clerical task or learning funtion. Hence, it is one good example to explain why any one successful person must need to own attempting to learn failure experience attitude in order to achieve his / her career plan more success, such as IBM founder , if he decided to continue to further his computer science degree, even he can graduate. He was only one common computer programmer in any one firm's computer department when IBM founder chose to do career decision to further to finish his computer science degree. Otherwise, he believed that global office and users can not apply computer softwares to do any clerical tasks in offices as well as global students can not apply computer softwares to type words on computer in order to finish their homeworks conveniently at homes. So, IBM founder can help us to apply computer typing skill to replace traditional writing word method successfully.

The another successful business founder is Amazon e-commerce founder. In his past life experience, he had been worlking in one software organization. He needed to help his clients to design different kinds of sotwares in order to satisfy themselves organizations needs. However, he felt that he dissatisfied his present job. He felt bored, he needed to find another new life changing experience. He planned to set up his new e-commerce organizational business. He planned to apply internet technology to let global any one buyer can apply interent tool to click mouse to his Amazon any one webstore to choose any one product to pay visa to buy at home conveniently. So, when one overseas buyer decides to buy one new smart phone, but the kind of new smart phone product can not been found to buy from the potential smart phone himself / herself domestic country's any one shop. When he /she applies internet to click to Amazon any one webstore, he /she saw this new kind of smart phone product photo, when he feels price is reasonable and he also likes this kind of new smartphone design, also because he / she can not find any one local smart phone product to buy in himself / herself country. So, Amazon can prvide good purchase channel to let this local smart phone buyer can buy this overseas new smart phone product from Amazon webstores at home conveniently.

IN fact, Amazon founder had this e-commerce business

plan. So, he have confidence to attempt and accept failure , such as if his e-commerce purchase method is not popular to be accepted to global any one product buyer. But, he knew that he must need to do choice, at the past time, either he chose to continue to do his software designer job or he forgave his present software designer job and he attempted to run his e-commerce new business. IN fact, I beleive that his new ecommerce founder aim, it does not focus on earning much profit and become rich businessman. His actual aim to let global any one buyer can turn on his /her computer to click to Amazon webstores to buy the kind of product when he /she can not find the kind of product in his/her local country. So, when the buyer can find the product from Amazon webstores, he / she can pays visa to buy the product . He /she does not need fly to overseas or wait the product to sell in his/her local country in future one day in possible.

Hence, " convenience purchase channel" mus tbe Amazon e-commerce organization mission objective. This objective is very important to influence Amazon future ecommerce organization continue success. Hence , Amazon founder has this objective to satisfy global buyers feel that they do not need to fly to foreign to buy any kinds of products when they can not buy in themselves countries easily. So this mission influences Amazon ec-mmerce business founder to forgive his past software designer job, due to his " internet convenient purchase channel " mission objective encourages he continue to pursue to improve his ecommerce online purchase delivery servicc needs to global any one e-buyer successfully. Hence, Amazon founder may be one good case to explain why he needs have learning failure experience to achieve presen his Amazon ecommerce organization to run successfully.